12804174

Taking Dyslexia to School

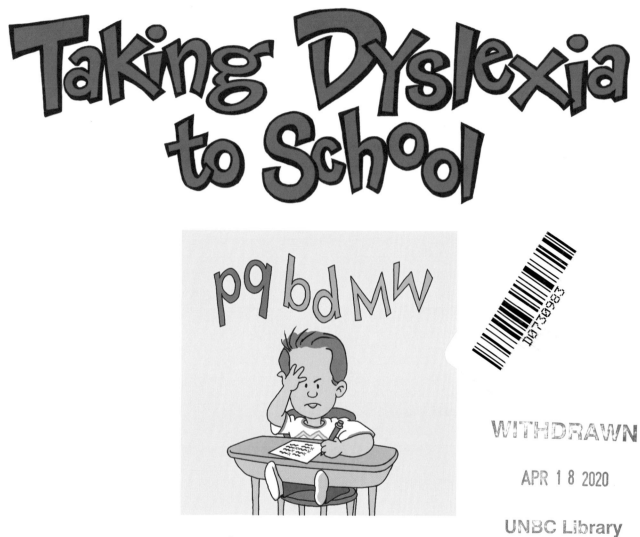

by Lauren E. Moynihan

Adapted for the Special Kids in School® series
created by Kim Gosselin

JayJo Books, L.L.C.
Publishing Special Books for Special Kids®

WITHDRAWN

APR 1 8 2020

UNBC Library

UNIVERSITY of NORTHERN
BRITISH COLUMBIA
LIBRARY
Prince George, B.C.

Taking Dyslexia to School
© 2002 JayJo Books, LLC
Edited by Karen Schader

All rights reserved. No part of this book may be reproduced or transmitted in any form or by any means, electronic or mechanical, including photocopying, recording, or by any information storage and retrieval system without written permission from the publisher. Printed in the United States of America.

Published by
JayJo Books, LLC
A Guidance Channel Company
Publishing Special Books for Special Kids®

JayJo Books is a publisher of books to help teachers, parents, and children cope with chronic illnesses, special needs, and health education in classroom, family, and social settings.

Library of Congress Control Number: 2001097487
ISBN 1-891383-17-5
First Edition
Eleventh book in our *Special Kids in School®* series

For information about
Premium and Special Sales, contact:
JayJo Books Special Sales Office
P.O. Box 213
Valley Park, MO 63088-0213
636-861-1331
jayjobooks@aol.com
www.jayjo.com

For all other information, contact:
JayJo Books
135 Dupont Street, P.O. Box 760
Plainview, NY 11803-0760
1-800-999-6884
jayjobooks@guidancechannel.com
www.jayjo.com

The opinions in this book are solely those of the author. Medical care is highly individualized and should never be altered without professional medical consultation.

Dedication

This book is dedicated to Tara Gorman.

About the Author

Lauren Moynihan was born and raised in Massachusetts. She currently lives in Brooklyn, New York and works as a lawyer.

She became interested in learning disabilities and special education while she was in law school. In law school, she represented children with learning and emotional disabilities, ensuring that they received appropriate educational placements. She also tutored children with learning disabilities.

Lauren was also inspired by her mother who works as a speech language pathologist and her friends with dyslexia who became accomplished lawyers.

Hi! My name is Matt, and I am a kid with dyslexia. Dyslexia is a kind of learning disability, which is a grown-up way of saying that sometimes it's hard for me to learn. There are lots of kinds of dyslexia. Some kids with dyslexia have trouble writing and spelling. I have trouble with reading and sometimes math. School is hard for lots of kids, but they don't all live with dyslexia.

You can't catch dyslexia from me or anyone else. I didn't do anything wrong to cause my dyslexia, and it's no one's fault either.

Having dyslexia doesn't mean I can't learn. My teacher says I'm very smart. But I didn't always think I was smart. Last year, it was really hard for me to read. It seemed like every other kid in class was reading better than me. Sometimes I got words mixed up. Some letters looked the same to me. Kids giggled when it was my turn to read.

When my teacher asked me questions, I could never seem to get the right words out even when I knew the answer.

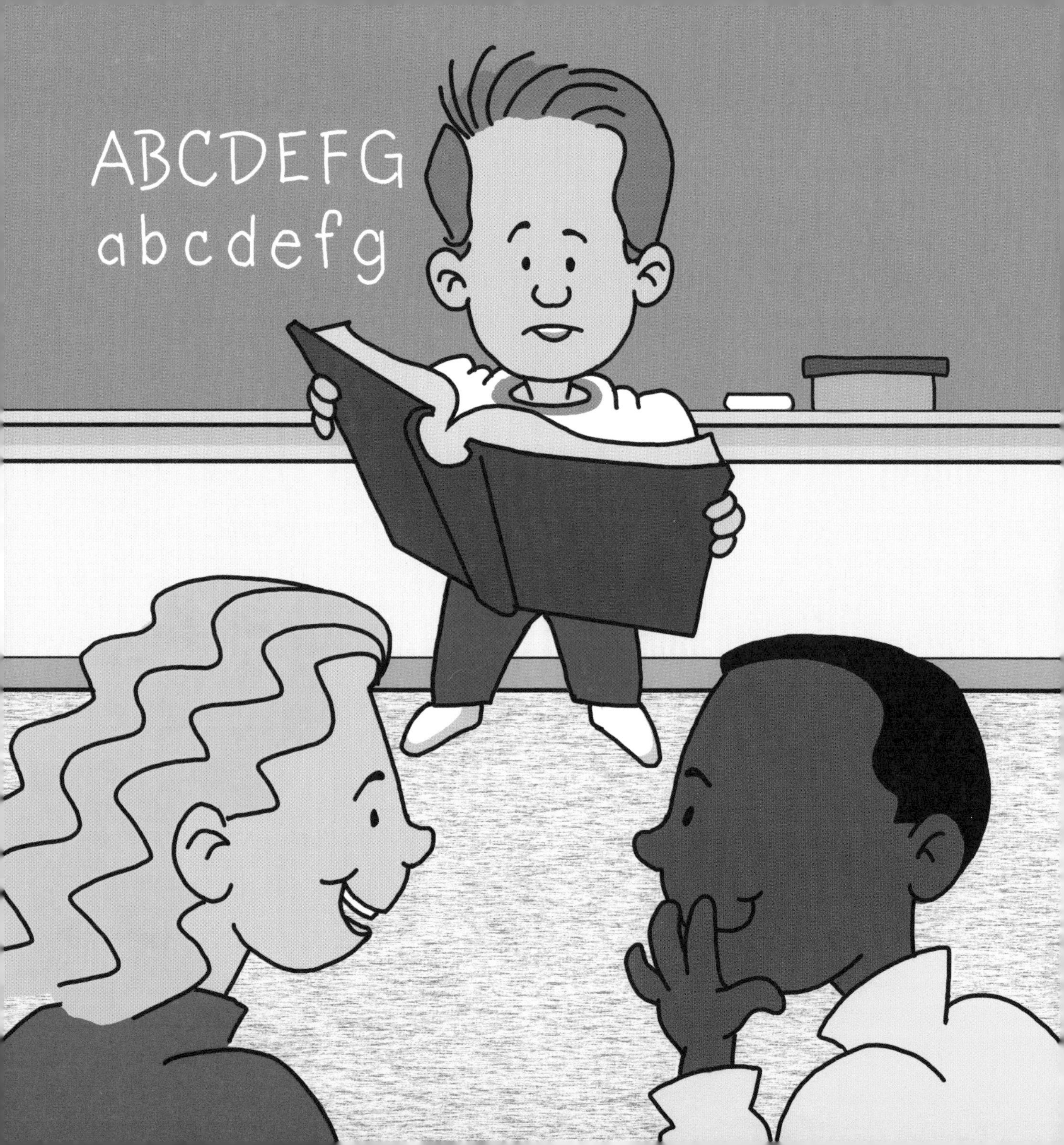
ABCDEFG
abcdefg

Spelling was hard for me too. Once I studied so hard for a spelling test, I missed my favorite TV show! When I got my test back, I had gotten most of the words wrong. My teacher told me to study harder.

How could I? I had already studied as hard as I could!

My mom knew that I worked hard in school. She said she used to have trouble in school too!

Mom read a paper the school sent home about kids with problems in school. It said there was a law that said schools had to give extra help to kids like me who have trouble learning. I was going to take a test to see if I had dyslexia.

I didn't want to take that test! I had enough trouble with tests in school.

I met with a lady called Ms. Jackson. She asked me so many questions, but I still liked her! She showed me a picture with lots of animals in it. I had to say the animals' names out loud as fast as I could. I was glad when Ms. Jackson said there were no wrong answers.

This test wasn't like the other tests I took at school. I even got a yo-yo when I was done!

After my test, my mom and I had a big meeting with Ms. Jackson. Ms. Jackson told us I had trouble reading because I had dyslexia. She said I had trouble understanding words, but that did not mean that I was not smart. Albert Einstein, a famous scientist, and Thomas Edison, the inventor of the light bulb, both had dyslexia!

Having dyslexia means my brain works differently. I have trouble reading, even though I am great at sports and art. Mom said it is like when our TV was broken. The picture was fuzzy on Channel 7. We couldn't hear the words on Channel 5, but Channel 4 worked fine.

Having dyslexia means that I have to work extra hard at school. With help from my parents and teachers, I can learn to read and write well too.

Now I have a special education teacher called Mr. Davis. We meet during reading time at school and three days a week after school. Mr. Davis teaches me all kinds of tricks to help me learn.

Mr. Davis showed me how to trace letters and numbers in the air to see how they are lined up. When I did this, I found that I had an easier time telling '6' from '9' and 'b' from 'd.' He also had posters in the room to remind me of how they look. Mr. Davis taught me how to break up words into sounds and blend sounds together to make words.

Even tapes can help with my reading! Now I listen to them while I read.

My mom helps me a lot at home too. We read together for an hour every night. She lets me pick the books we read. After we read, Mom and I talk about the story. My favorite story was about a famous artist named Michelangelo who also had dyslexia.

Last year, I never thought reading could be so much fun!

Mr. Davis talked to my other teachers about ways to make it easier for me to learn. Now I use graph paper to help me do my math. I still read slower than most kids, so I get extra time to finish my tests. Sometimes Mr. Davis reads my tests out loud to me. I get to do a lot of my work on the computer too!

Dyslexia doesn't stop me from learning new things. Sometimes I just need extra time to finish my schoolwork.

I have to work hard at school, but I still have lots of time to play and be with my friends. My friend Max is really smart. He is my special study partner. We do schoolwork every afternoon. I still love to play computer games and baseball, though. My mom even signed me up for the soccer team next year!

Now I do really well in school. Other kids say that I am smart. I love hearing that!

Mr. Davis told me he has a friend who lives with dyslexia. His friend is a lawyer. Lawyers have to read and write a lot. With hard work and help from my teachers, maybe I can even read and write that well someday!

Even though I have dyslexia, I know I can be anything I want to be when I grow up.

LET'S TAKE THE DYSLEXIA KIDS' QUIZ!

1. What is dyslexia?
Dyslexia is called a 'learning disability.' Kids with dyslexia often have trouble with reading, writing and spelling.

2. Can kids with dyslexia be smart?
Yes! Dyslexia has nothing to do with being smart.

3. Name some famous people who had dyslexia.
Albert Einstein, Thomas Edison, Michelangelo... and many others!

4. Can people with dyslexia play sports and do other activities?
Yes. People with dyslexia may be gifted in other areas such as sports, art, music, computers, drama, and music.

5. Can you catch dyslexia?
No. Dyslexia is not contagious.

6. If you have dyslexia, does that mean that you are lazy?
No. Kids with dyslexia have trouble reading and writing. Sometimes they have trouble doing schoolwork. That doesn't mean they are lazy or not trying hard.

7. Can kids with dyslexia learn to read and write?

Kids with dyslexia can learn to read and write like most other kids. They may just need a little extra time or special help.

8. Do schools help kids with learning disabilities?

Yes! Our government wants to be sure that kids with learning disabilities get a good education. They passed a law that says kids with learning disabilities should get extra help.

9. What are some ways kids with dyslexia can get help in school?

They can use books on tape.
They can use flash cards.
They can write on the computer.
They can use graph paper for math.

10. Why do kids with dyslexia sometimes get more time to take a test?

Because of their learning disability, kids with dyslexia often need extra time for their tests.

Great job! Thanks for taking the Dyslexia Kids' Quiz!

TEN TIPS FOR TEACHERS

✔ **1. EACH CHILD WITH DYSLEXIA IS UNIQUE.**

Dyslexia varies in severity and impacts each person differently. The most common manifestations of dyslexia are problems in reading, writing, and spelling. Students with dyslexia may also experience problems learning to speak, organizing spoken and written language, learning letters and their sounds, memorizing number facts, or performing math operations. Some students do not have problems with early reading and writing, but experience problems when language skills become more complex.

✔ **2. BE AWARE OF THE COMMON SYMPTOMS OF DYSLEXIA IN EARLY GRADES.**

In primary school, a number of different factors are indicative of dyslexia. Some of these factors include: difficulty in decoding single words; inability to identify "sight words"; awkwardness in pencil grip; consistent reading and spelling errors, including letter reversals, word reversals, inversion, transpositions, substitutions; slowness in learning the connection between letters and sounds. Younger children may show language delays or articulation problems.

✔ **3. EARLY TESTING IS IMPERATIVE FOR STUDENTS WITH DYSLEXIA.**

If you suspect a student has dyslexia, it is important to have the student evaluated. Testing is the only way to diagnose dyslexia. Although dyslexia is the most common reading disability, problems in reading stem from other disorders. An assessment can determine whether learning problems are related to dyslexia, other disorders, or a combination of disorders. Early detection and treatment is essential to help children learn to read at grade level.

✔ **4. STUDENTS LIVING WITH DYSLEXIA MAY NEED ASSISTANCE WITH EMOTIONAL ISSUES.**

These students may have already experienced failure at school, and their self-esteem may be fragile. After a history of academic problems, a student may be discouraged. Mental health specialists may be necessary to help students cope with their problems, but teachers can foster self-esteem by praising areas in which the student succeeds (such as sports or artwork) or improves. It is also important to praise a child's effort and persistence.

✔ **5. APPLY A TEAM APPROACH TO TEACHING.**

Communicate with the student's parents, caregivers, special education teachers, speech pathologists, psychologists and any other individuals who are working with the child. The key to working with a child with dyslexia is communication to ensure that all individuals are using a united approach to teaching the child. Consider giving the student with dyslexia a peer study partner (someone the student is already friends with) to help them learn.

6. ACADEMIC MODIFICATIONS MAY BE NECESSARY TO HELP STUDENTS WITH DYSLEXIA SUCCEED.

Students with dyslexia should not be penalized. Various modifications in instruction and testing can help them succeed. These students may need additional time to complete tasks and take tests. They may benefit from having lessons and books on tape, taking exams or completing assignments on computer, or using graph paper to help them organize their thoughts. Multisensory teaching, which involves using visual, auditory, and kinesthetic-tactile methods simultaneously, has proven effective in helping students with dyslexia decode language.

7. STUDENTS LIVING WITH DYSLEXIA BENEFIT FROM HAVING A HIGHLY ORGANIZED CLASSROOM.

Keeping noise levels and clutter down in the classroom helps students with dyslexia. Have an outline on the blackboard describing the lesson plan for the period or the day. Have homework assignments clearly written on the board. When teaching a new idea or concept, use the "spiral back" technique. This means giving students the main idea before addressing the concept in detail and then repeating the main idea at the end of the lesson.

8. DO NOT CALL ON A STUDENT LIVING WITH DYSLEXIA TO READ OUT LOUD.

Students with dyslexia have particular difficulty with reading out loud in class or spontaneously answering questions. Agree on a plan with the student that can reduce anxiety. Tell the student you will not call on them unless their hand is raised or you are standing in a particular spot in the classroom. A plan can help the child prepare for your questions.

9. STUDENTS WITH DYSLEXIA MAY ALSO HAVE DYSGRAPHIA OR WRITING DISABILITIES.

Many of these students also have problems with dysgraphia or difficulty with handwriting. Like dyslexia, dysgraphia manifests itself in a number of different ways. Proper instruction will depend on the student. Muscle training and overlearning good techniques for letter formation are critical. Students often respond well to writing words with their eyes closed, or kinesthetic writing. Many students also benefit from using a word processor or computer for assignments and tests.

10. BE AWARE OF THE LEGAL RIGHTS OF YOUR STUDENTS.

The Individuals with Disabilities in Education Act establishes that schools have to provide a free appropriate public education to students with learning disabilities. Take appropriate action if a student needs to be tested. Do your best to adapt teaching methods to meet the needs of any student with a learning disability. You are an important role model and your efforts will be greatly rewarded!

ADDiTiONAL RESOURCES

National Center for Learning Disabilities
381 Park Avenue South Suite 1401
New York, NY 10016
212-545-7510
888-575-7373
www.ld.org

Learning Disabilities Association of America
(LDA)
4156 Library Road
Pittsburgh, PA 15234-1349
412-341-1515
888-300-6710
www.ldanatl.org

International Dyslexia Association (IDA)
8600 LaSalle Road
Chester Building, Suite 382
Baltimore, MD 21286-2044
410-296-0232
800-222-3123
www.interdys.org

**National Institute of Child Health and
Human Development (NICHD)**
P.O. Box 3006
Rockville, MD 20847
800-370-2943
www.nichd.nih.gov

Dyslexia Research Institute
5746 Centerville Road
Tallahassee, FL 32308
850-893-2216
www.dyslexia-add.org

To order additional copies of *Taking Dyslexia to School* or inquire about our quantity discounts for schools, hospitals, and affiliated organizations, contact us at 1-800-999-6884.

From our *Special Kids in School®* series
Taking A.D.D. to School
Taking Asthma to School
Taking Autism to School
Taking Cancer to School
Taking Cerebral Palsy to School
Taking Cystic Fibrosis to School
Taking Diabetes to School
Taking Down Syndrome to School
Taking Food Allergies to School
Taking Seizure Disorders to School
Taking Tourette Syndrome to School
...and others coming soon!

From our new *Healthy Habits for Kids®* series
There's a Louse in My House
A Fun Story about Kids and Head Lice

From our new *Special Family and Friends™* series
Allie Learns About Alzheimer's Disease
A Family Story about Love, Patience, and Acceptance
Patrick Learns About Parkinson's Disease
A Story of a Special Bond Between Friends
... and others coming soon!

And from our *Substance Free Kids®* series
Smoking STINKS!!™
A Heartwarming Story about the Importance of Avoiding Tobacco

Other books available now!
SPORTSercise!
A School Story about
Exercise-Induced Asthma
ZooAllergy
A Fun Story about Allergy
and Asthma Triggers
Rufus Comes Home
Rufus the Bear with Diabetes™
A Story about Diagnosis and Acceptance
The ABC's of Asthma
An Asthma Alphabet Book
for Kids of All Ages
Taming the Diabetes Dragon
A Story about Living Better
with Diabetes
Trick-or-Treat for Diabetes
A Halloween Story for Kids
Living with Diabetes

A portion of the proceeds from all our publications is donated to various charities to help fund important medical research and education. We work hard to make a difference in the lives of children with chronic conditions and/or special needs. Thank you for your support.